Kit and the Magic Kite

Helen Cooper

Hamish Hamilton · London

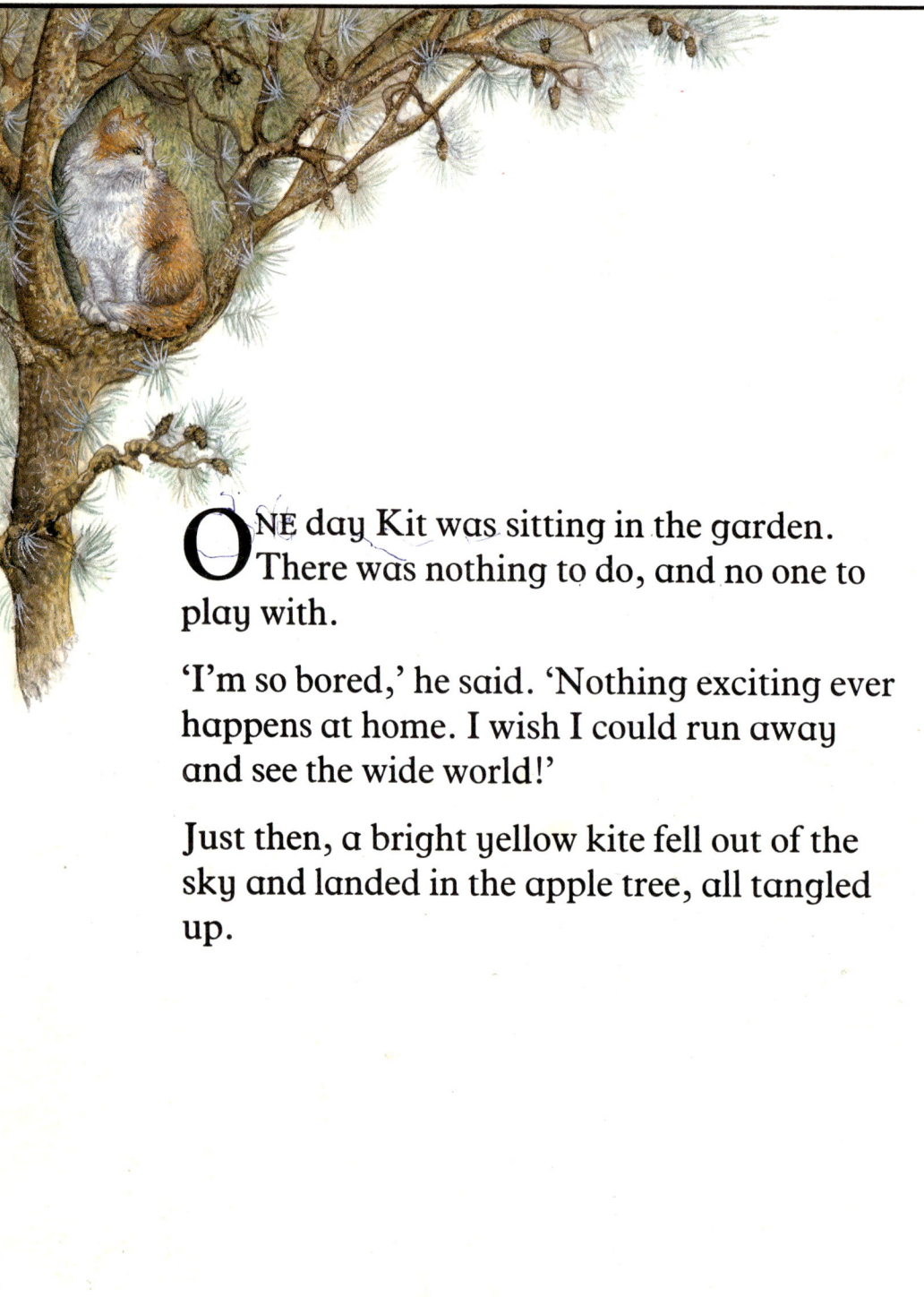

ONE day Kit was sitting in the garden. There was nothing to do, and no one to play with.

'I'm so bored,' he said. 'Nothing exciting ever happens at home. I wish I could run away and see the wide world!'

Just then, a bright yellow kite fell out of the sky and landed in the apple tree, all tangled up.

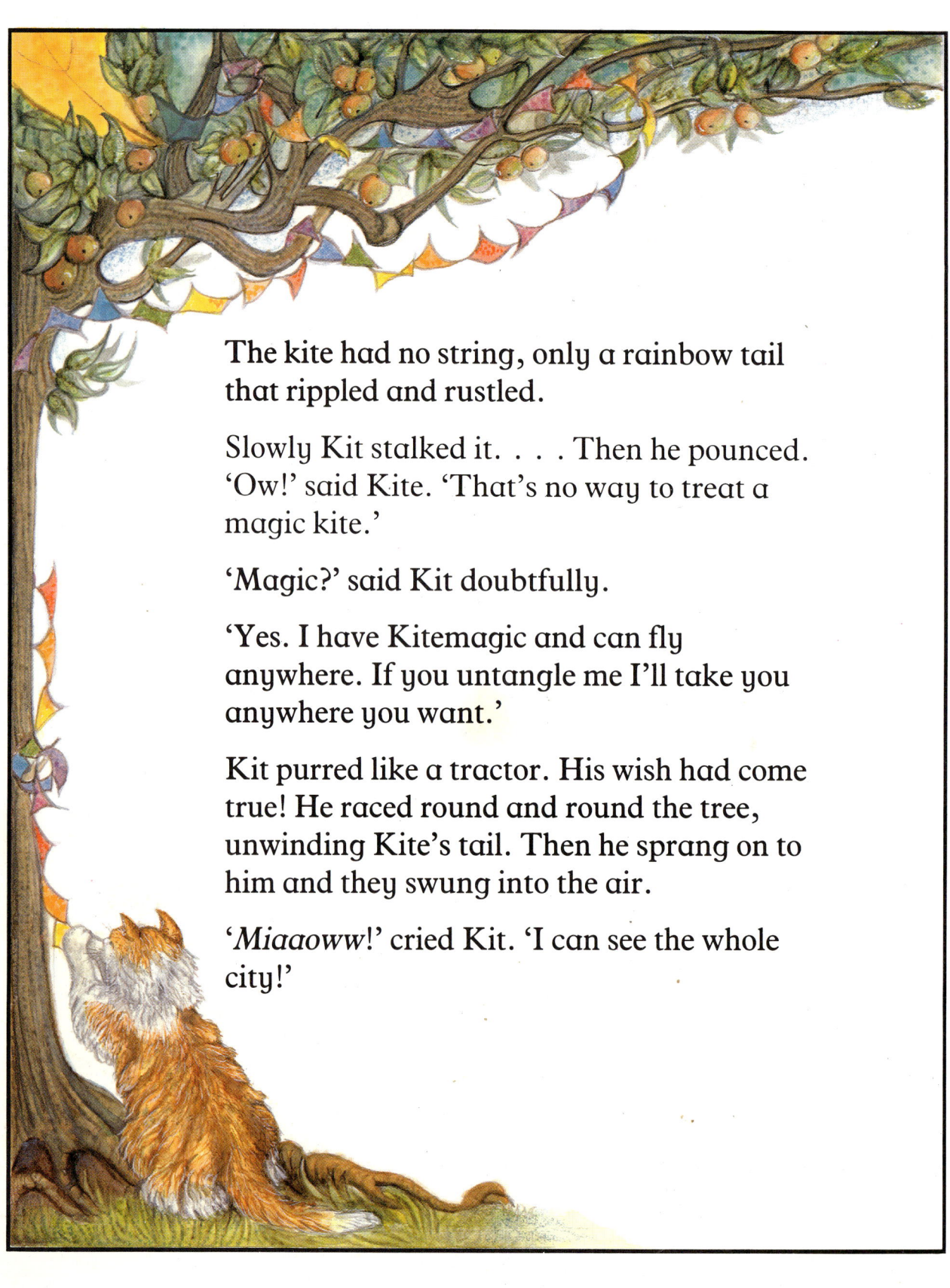

The kite had no string, only a rainbow tail that rippled and rustled.

Slowly Kit stalked it. . . . Then he pounced. 'Ow!' said Kite. 'That's no way to treat a magic kite.'

'Magic?' said Kit doubtfully.

'Yes. I have Kitemagic and can fly anywhere. If you untangle me I'll take you anywhere you want.'

Kit purred like a tractor. His wish had come true! He raced round and round the tree, unwinding Kite's tail. Then he sprang on to him and they swung into the air.

'*Miaaoww!*' cried Kit. 'I can see the whole city!'

'Let's land!' said Kit. 'I can be an alley-cat!'

So down they sank, until Kit could climb on to a chimney-pot.

'I'll be ready when you want me,' said Kite.

'I won't want you for weeks,' Kit purred. 'I'm going to be King of the Alley-Cats.'
And Kit marched happily over the rooftops.

The starlings weren't so happy. When they saw Kit they swooped out and flapped their wings in his face.

Kit snarled and pawed the air bravely, but then he ran quickly down the drain-pipe into the alley below.

Kit was hungry. 'Mmm, I smell kippers,' he said, as he peered inside an open dustbin.

Suddenly he heard a low snarl and an angry hiss.

Kit's fur bristled. He spun round and saw three huge warrior cats with fiery eyes and battle scars. Kit backed away as they came nearer. Then he turned and bolted back up the drain-pipe.

Luckily Kite was waiting and Kit scrambled up. Off they flew, leaving the city behind them.

'That was a short week,' smirked Kite. 'How did you like being King of the Alley-Cats?'

Kit washed himself, pretending he hadn't heard. When he finished he sat up.
'Who wants to be an alley-cat, anyway? I want to be a wildcat and hunt my own food. Let's land in those woods below.'

So down they went. Kit leaped on to the branch of a tall tree.

'I'll be ready when you're hungry,' said Kite.

'I won't be hungry here,' said Kit.

Kit came down from the tree by the quickest way he knew. Then he crawled his way through the undergrowth towards the stream.

'I'm a Fierce Wildcat,' he said, 'and I'm going to catch lots of fish.'

Kit flicked his paw into the water. But he didn't catch anything. He flicked again. After fifty flicks Kit wasn't sure if he liked fishing.

Then a real wildcat came out of the trees and crouched by the stream. He caught ten fish straight away.

'You rrrreally ought to catch something,' said Wildcat. 'You'll be hungrrrry later on.'

Kit tried again, but by now his paw was cold and numb.

When Kite sailed back over the tree tops, Kit was very happy to see him.

'Had enough fish, then?' said Kite.
'No, I haven't,' wailed Kit. 'I've decided it's best for cats to be fed. Now a ship's cat would have fish every day, *and* see exciting things.'

'To sea, then,' said Kite.

Soon they were skimming over the waves.

'Ship ahoy!' said Kite.

As they came closer they saw a bright orange cat sitting on the mast. It looked friendly.

'Permission to land?' called Kite.

'Permission granted,' said the orange cat.

'I be Captain Scarlet,' said the ship's cat. 'I give the orders around here.'

'Aye, Aye, Captain,' said Kit, following Captain Scarlet down a ladder into a dark cabin, full of sacks.

'Keep still and listen for rats,' hissed Captain Scarlet.

Kit kept still. But the floor didn't. It jerked up and down in a most peculiar way. Kit felt sick.

Suddenly there was a rustle. A rat ran out from beneath the sacks.

'Go for it!' hissed Captain Scarlet.

Kit pounced . . . but he felt so dizzy he fell over.

Captain Scarlet caught the rat. 'You haven't got your sea-legs yet,' he said. 'As it's your first day, I'll let you off. Come up on deck.'

Captain Scarlet and Kit sat in the stern outside, watching the fishermen pull in the nets. The men threw them a fish each, but poor Kit felt too sick to eat his.

'Stand on the edge and you'll get more air,' ordered Captain Scarlet.

So Kit did.

Then the wind changed. The boat lurched to one side. A big wave hit the boat and Kit was falling – down . . . down . . . down . . . .

Just as he went under, Kite dived in and dragged him up.

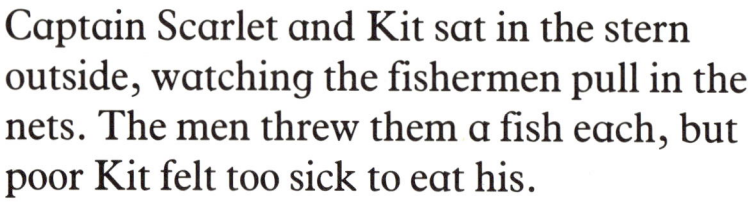

Away they flew, into the moonlit sky.

Suddenly three figures whirled out of the night – witches!

'Miaaoww, now I can become a witch's cat!' shouted Kit.

'Hold on, then,' groaned Kite.
Up and up they swooshed.

'Who are you?' snapped the Chief Witch.

'I've come to be a witch's cat.'

The other cats sniggered.
'A new servant!' grinned the Witch greedily. 'My cat Grimble needs help, you'd better follow us.'

Her witchy friends all winked and cackled.

Down they swooped to a crooked little house, deep in the middle of a dark forest. Kit slowly followed Grimble and the grinning Witch inside. He wasn't sure if he still wanted to be a witch's cat.

'Clean this house by daybreak, or you'll get no food,' the Witch cackled, and disappeared.

'Let's start work,' said Kit. 'I'm so hungry.'

'There won't be anything but sour milk,' groaned Grimble. 'I'd escape, if I were you, before she casts a spell to make you stay forever.'

'Miaaoww! Casts a spell!'

In the flickering candlelight, Kit saw the Witch stirring a murky potion in her cauldron. Under her breath she was muttering strange-sounding words. Kit's fur stood on end. Quickly he scrambled through a broken window to freedom.

Kite was outside, chatting to the broomstick.

'Quick, take me away!' whimpered Kit. 'I want to be with kind humans.'

Kite scooped Kit up and they soared away, gliding down at last to a familiar garden.

Kit's friends were a little suspicious about his adventures.
'I was King of the Alley-Cats!' Kit boasted. 'And the Fiercest Wildcat, and the Captain's ship cat, *and* the Chief Witch's cat! Ask Kite if you don't believe me!'

But when Kit looked up, all he could see in the sky was a black speck with a long, bright tail. Kite was waving good-bye.

To my parents and Brian

First published in Great Britain in 1987
by Hamish Hamilton Children's Books
27 Wrights Lane, London W8 5TZ
Copyright © 1987 by Helen Cooper
All rights reserved

British Library Cataloguing in Publication Data
Cooper, Helen
Kit and kite magic.
I. Title
823'.914[J]   PZ7
ISBN 0–241–11987–1

Typeset by Kalligraphics Ltd
Printed in Great Britain by Cambus Litho and
bound by Hunter & Foulis Ltd